Designed and Published by Simon Creedy
(simon@creedy.com.au)

WORDS OF GOD

PRAYERS AND
HOLY WRITINGS
FROM

Bahá'u'lláh
The Báb

AND

'Abdu'l-Bahá

Do not be
content
with
showing
friendship in words
alone, let your heart
burn with loving
kindness for all
who may cross
your path.

'Abdu'l Bahá

BAHÁ'U'LLÁH (1817-1892)

THE DIVINE EDUCATOR

In the middle of the 19th century, God summoned Bahá'u'lláh–meaning the "Glory of God"–to deliver a new Revelation to humanity. For four decades thousands of verses, letters and books flowed from His pen. In His Writings, He outlined a framework for the development of a global civilization which takes into account both the spiritual and material dimensions of human life.

I have never aspired after worldly leadership. My sole purpose hath been to hand down unto men that which I was bidden to deliver by God...

– Bahá'u'lláh

Bahá'u'lláh suffered 40 years of imprisonment, torture and exile for bringing God's latest message to humanity. Today, His life and mission are becoming increasingly well-known across the planet. Millions of people are learning to apply His teachings to their individual and collective lives for the betterment of the world.

The Shrine of Bahá'u'lláh, located in Bahjí near Akka, Israel, is the holiest place for Bahá'ís and represents their Qiblih, or direction of prayer. It contains the remains of Bahá'u'lláh and is near the spot where He died in the Mansion of Bahjí.

THE BÁB (1819-1850)

HERALD OF THE BAHÁ'Í FAITH

In the middle of the 19th century–one of the most turbulent periods in the world's history–a young merchant announced that He was the bearer of a message destined to transform the life of humanity. At a time when His country, Iran, was undergoing widespread moral breakdown, His message aroused excitement and hope among all classes, rapidly attracting thousands of followers. He took the name "The Báb", meaning "the Gate" in Arabic.

With His call for spiritual and moral reformation, and His attention to improving the position of women and the lot of the poor, the Báb's prescription for spiritual renewal was revolutionary. At the same time, He founded a distinct, independent religion of His own, inspiring His followers to transform their lives and carry out great acts of heroism.

The Báb announced that humanity stood at the threshold of a new era. His mission, which was to last only six years, was to prepare the way for the coming of a Manifestation of God Who would usher in the age of peace and justice promised in all the world's religions: Bahá'u'lláh.

Shrine of The Báb, Mount Carmel, Haifa, Israel

ʿABDUʾL-BAHÁ (1844-1921)

THE PERFECT EXEMPLAR

In the early years of the 20th century, ʿAbduʾl-Bahá—the eldest Son of Baháʾuʾlláh—was the Baháʾí Faith's leading exponent, renowned as a champion of social justice and an ambassador for international peace.

Upholding unity as the fundamental principle of His teachings, Baháʾuʾlláh established the necessary safeguard to ensure that His religion would never suffer the same fate as others that split into sects after the deaths of their Founders. In His Writings, He instructed all to turn to His eldest Son, ʿAbduʾl-Bahá, not only as the authorized interpreter of the Baháʾí Writings but also as the perfect exemplar of the Faith's spirit and teachings.

Following Baháʾuʾlláh's passing, ʿAbduʾl-Bahá's extraordinary qualities of character, His knowledge and His service to humanity offered a vivid demonstration of Baháʾuʾlláh's teachings in action, and brought great prestige to the rapidly expanding community throughout the world.

ʿAbduʾl-Bahá devoted His ministry to furthering His Father's Faith and to promoting the ideals of peace and unity. He encouraged the establishment of local Baháʾí institutions, and guided nascent educational, social and economic initiatives. After His release from a lifetime of imprisonment, ʿAbduʾl-Bahá set out on a series of journeys which took Him to Egypt, Europe and North America. Throughout His life, He presented with brilliant simplicity, to high and low alike, Baháʾuʾlláh's prescription for the spiritual and social renewal of society.

Shrine of ʿAbduʾl-Bahá close to the Ridván Garden in Akka, Israel

Is there any Remover of difficulties save God?
Say: Praised be God!
He is God!
All are His servants,
and all abide by
His bidding!

The Báb

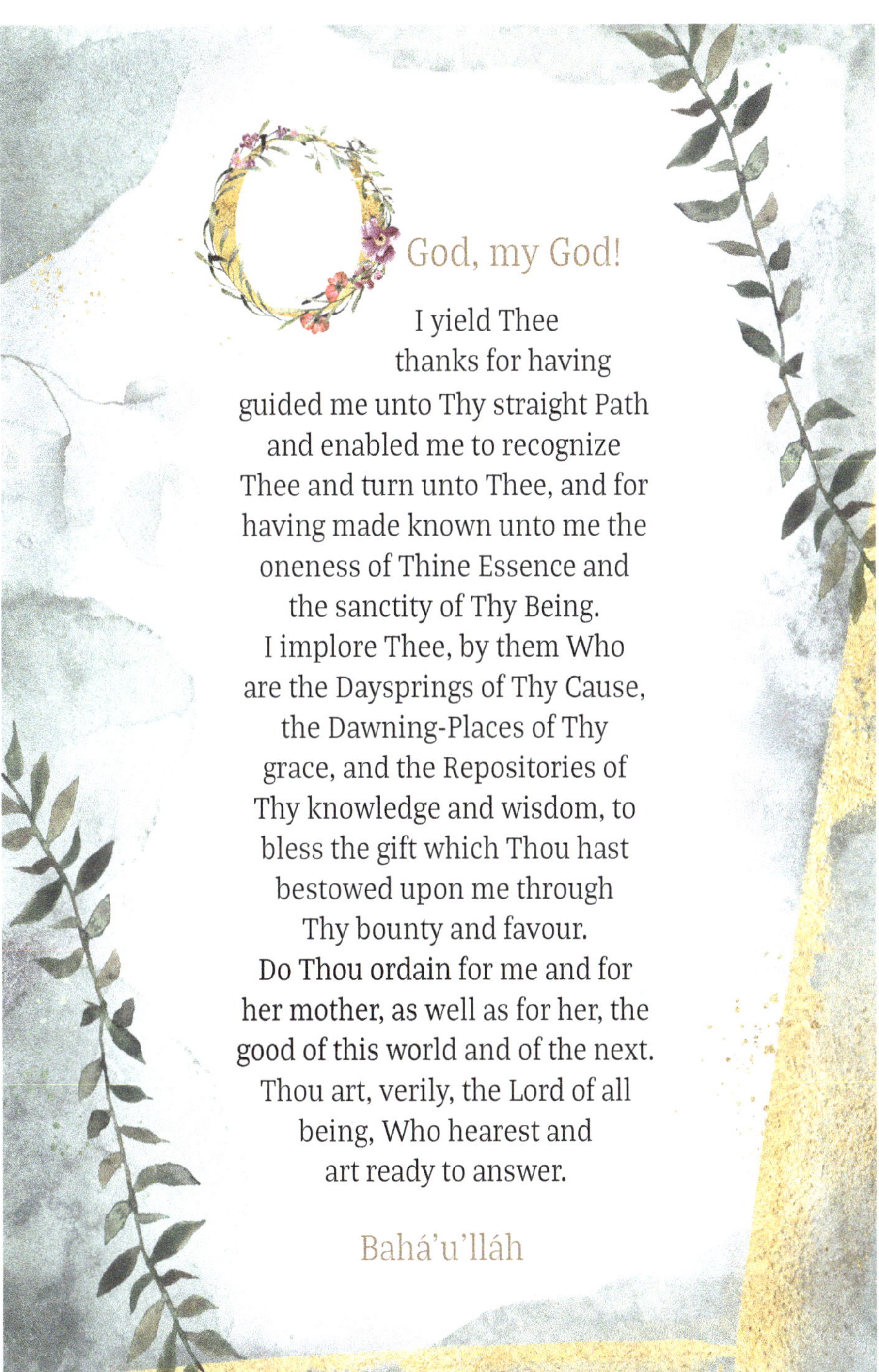

Revealed for the recipient on the occasion of the birth of his daughter

Thy name is
my healing,
O my God, and
remembrance
of Thee is
my remedy.
Nearness to Thee
is my hope,
and love for Thee
is my companion.
Thy mercy to me
is my healing
and my succor
in both this world
and the world
to come.
Thou, verily, art
the All-Bountiful,
the All-Knowing,
the All-Wise.

Bahá'u'lláh

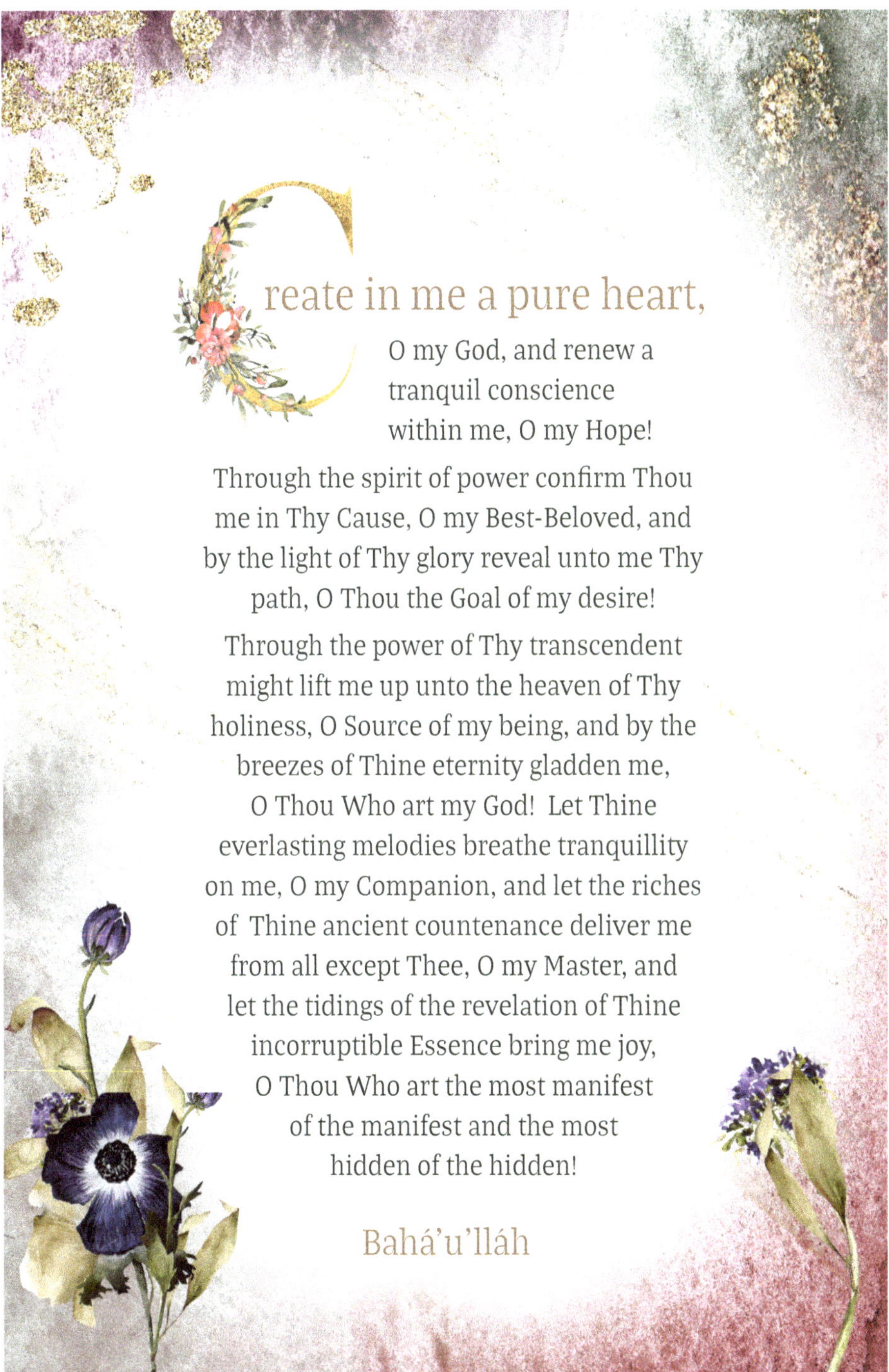

Create in me a pure heart,

O my God, and renew a
tranquil conscience
within me, O my Hope!

Through the spirit of power confirm Thou
me in Thy Cause, O my Best-Beloved, and
by the light of Thy glory reveal unto me Thy
path, O Thou the Goal of my desire!

Through the power of Thy transcendent
might lift me up unto the heaven of Thy
holiness, O Source of my being, and by the
breezes of Thine eternity gladden me,
O Thou Who art my God! Let Thine
everlasting melodies breathe tranquillity
on me, O my Companion, and let the riches
of Thine ancient countenance deliver me
from all except Thee, O my Master, and
let the tidings of the revelation of Thine
incorruptible Essence bring me joy,
O Thou Who art the most manifest
of the manifest and the most
hidden of the hidden!

Bahá'u'lláh

Blessed is
the spot,
and the house,
and the place,
and the city,
and the heart,
and the mountain,
and the refuge,
and the cave,
and the valley,
and the land,
and the sea,
and the island,
and the meadow
where mention of God
hath been made,
and His praise
glorified.

Bahá'u'lláh

O
God,
guide me,
protect me,
make of me
a shining lamp
and a
brilliant star.
Thou art
the Mighty
and the
Powerful.

'Abdu'l-Bahá

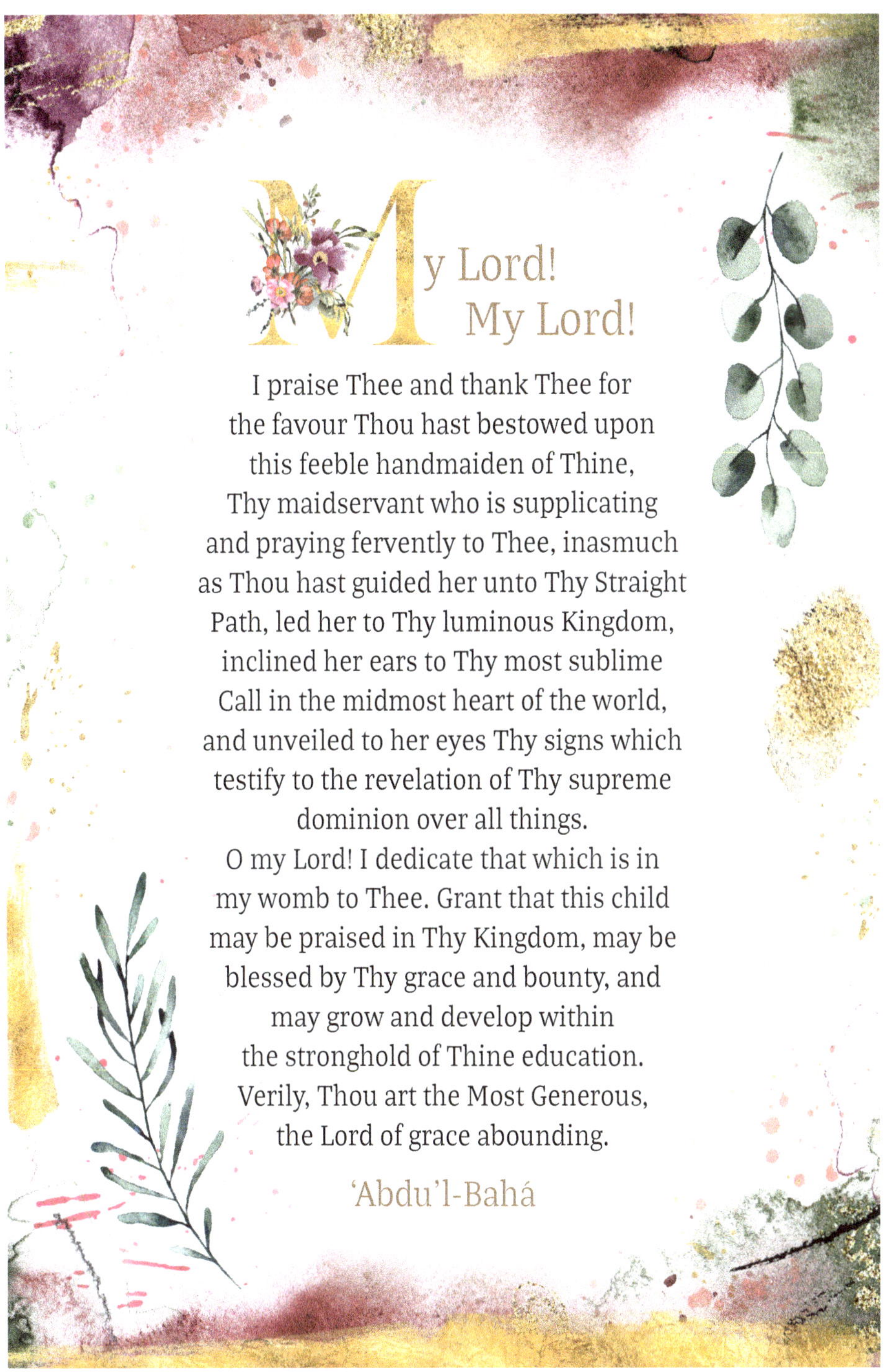

My Lord! My Lord!

I praise Thee and thank Thee for
the favour Thou hast bestowed upon
this feeble handmaiden of Thine,
Thy maidservant who is supplicating
and praying fervently to Thee, inasmuch
as Thou hast guided her unto Thy Straight
Path, led her to Thy luminous Kingdom,
inclined her ears to Thy most sublime
Call in the midmost heart of the world,
and unveiled to her eyes Thy signs which
testify to the revelation of Thy supreme
dominion over all things.
O my Lord! I dedicate that which is in
my womb to Thee. Grant that this child
may be praised in Thy Kingdom, may be
blessed by Thy grace and bounty, and
may grow and develop within
the stronghold of Thine education.
Verily, Thou art the Most Generous,
the Lord of grace abounding.

‘Abdu’l-Bahá

Make my prayer
O my Lord,
a fountain of living waters
whereby I may live as
long as Thy sovereignty
endureth, and may make
mention of Thee in every
world of Thy worlds.

Bahá'u'lláh

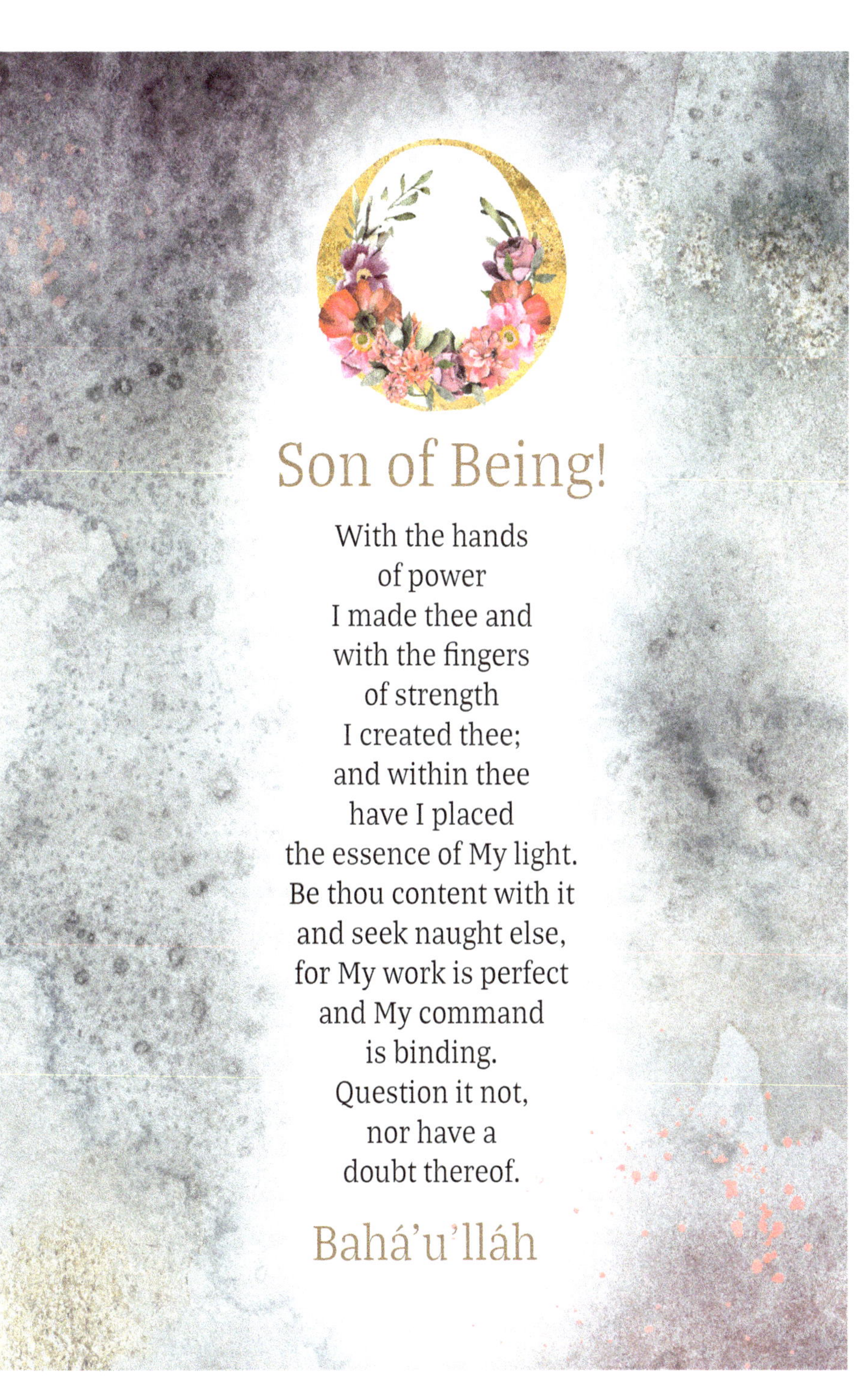

Son of Being!

With the hands
of power
I made thee and
with the fingers
of strength
I created thee;
and within thee
have I placed
the essence of My light.
Be thou content with it
and seek naught else,
for My work is perfect
and My command
is binding.
Question it not,
nor have a
doubt thereof.

Bahá'u'lláh

Let us put aside
all thoughts
of self;
let us close our eyes
to all on earth,
let us neither
make known
our sufferings
nor complain of
our wrongs.
Rather let us
become oblivious
of our own selves,
and drinking down
the wine of
heavenly grace,
let us cry out our joy,
and lose ourselves
in the beauty
of the
All-Glorious.

'Abdu'l-Bahá

O Son
of
Spirit!

My first
counsel is
this: Possess
a pure, kindly
and radiant
heart, that
thine may be
a sovereignty
ancient,
imperishable
and
everlasting.

Bahá'u'lláh

Son
of Being!

Busy not
thyself with
this world, for
with fire We
test the gold,
and with gold
We test Our
servants.

Bahá'u'lláh

O
My
Friend
in Word!

Ponder awhile.
Hast thou ever
heard that
friend and foe
should abide
in one heart?
Cast out then
the stranger,
that the Friend
may enter His
home.

Bahá'u'lláh

O Son of Being!

Love Me,
that I may
love thee.
If thou lovest
Me not,
My love can
in no wise
reach thee.
Know this,
O servant.

Bahá'u'lláh

Son
of Man!

For everything
there is a sign.
The sign of love
is fortitude
under
My decree and
patience under
My trials.

Bahá'u'lláh

Son of Being!
Make mention of Me on My earth, that in My heaven I may remember thee, thus shall Mine eyes and thine be solaced.
Bahá'u'lláh

O

My Servant!

Free thyself
from the fetters
of this world,
and loose thy
soul from
the prison of
self. Seize thy
chance, for it
will come
to thee
no more.

Bahá'u'lláh

Man of
Two Visions!

Close one eye
and open the other.
Close one to the world
and all that is therein,
and open the
other to the
hallowed beauty
of the Beloved.

Bahá'u'lláh

O Son of
Justice!
Whither can
a lover go but
to the land of his beloved?
and what seeker findeth
rest away from his
heart's desire?
To the true lover
reunion is life,
and separation
is death.
His breast is void of
patience and his heart
hath no peace.
A myriad lives he would
forsake to hasten to the
abode of his beloved.

Bahá'u'lláh

Son of Being!

Thou art My lamp and
My light is in thee.
Get thou from it thy
radiance and seek
none other than Me.
For I have created
thee rich and have
bountifully shed
My favour
upon thee.

Bahá'u'lláh

When a thought of war comes, oppose it by a stronger thought of peace.

A thought of hatred must be destroyed by a more powerful thought of love.

'Abdu'l-Bahá

He is the All-Glorious!

O God, my God! Lowly and tearful, I raise my suppliant hands to Thee and cover my face in the dust of that Threshold of Thine, exalted above the knowledge of the learned, and the praise of all that glorify Thee. Graciously look upon Thy servant, humble and lowly at Thy door, with the glances of the eye of Thy mercy, and immerse him in the Ocean of Thine eternal grace. Lord! He is a poor and lowly servant of Thine, enthralled and imploring Thee, captive in Thy hand, praying fervently to Thee, trusting in Thee, in tears before Thy face, calling to Thee and beseeching Thee, saying: O Lord, my God! Give me Thy grace to serve Thy loved ones, strengthen me in my servitude to Thee, illumine my brow with the light of adoration in Thy court of holiness, and of prayer to Thy kingdom of grandeur. Help me to be selfless at the heavenly entrance of Thy gate, and aid me to be detached from all things within Thy holy precincts. Lord! Give me to drink from the chalice of selflessness; with its robe clothe me, and in its ocean immerse me. Make me as dust in the pathway of Thy loved ones, and grant that I may offer up my soul for the earth ennobled by the footsteps of Thy chosen ones in Thy path, O Lord of Glory in the Highest. With this prayer doth Thy servant call Thee, at dawntide and in the night-season. Fulfill his heart's desire, O Lord! Illumine his heart, gladden his bosom, kindle his light, that he may serve Thy Cause and Thy servants. Thou art the Bestower, the Pitiful, the Most Bountiful, the Gracious, the Merciful, the Compassionate.

'Abdu'l-Bahá

9 781922 562470